This book

belongs

to

Lets Uncomplicate Life

Intricate is defi ned as something having many interrelated parts or facets; entan- gled or involved. Is this not what our lives have become? When I looked around me I found that everybody has created complications which can be avoided with little effort - especially in relationships. Then a natural question comes: How do you untangle stuff or make it less intricate? Well there are many ways to this like meditation, yoga, gardening, running etc. etc. Each one has his or her own way of relaxing for me its drawing coloring pages. If one of your relaxing ways is coloring, then this book is for you.

This book tries to untangle those complicated things in life through the relaxing power of coloring. The thought of each drawing is printed at the opposite page.

I hope these Intricate designs bring as much joy to you in coloring as they brought to me while creating. I would to love to see how the designs come out after coloring, please share them at Instagram with #intrikateink or tag me @in- trikateink. Grab your colors, play your favorite music and enjoy. If you have any questions or simply want to say hello you can always reach me at surabhikuthiala@gmail.com

Love, Surabhi

"It is only when you are pursued that you become swift." ~ khalil Gibran

"Happiness is something that multiplies
when it is divided." ~Paulo Coelho.

"Holding onto anger is like drinking poison and expecting the other person to die." - Anonymous.

"My demons tried to drown me, but they didn't know I could breathe underwater"

- Jordan Sarah Weatherhead

"I still have a long way to go, but I'm already so far from where I used to be, and I'm proud of that" - Anonymous

"Beauty is power; a smile is its sword"

- John Ray

"I'm not shy I'm just holding back my awesomeness so I won't intimidate you." - Anonymous

"Pursue some path, however narrow and crooked, in which you can walk with love and reverence." - Henry David Thoreau

"I play bass. I don't have to go out there and screech." - Tina Waymouth

"Prayer alone will overcome the gigantic difficulties." -John Mott

"When your legs get tired, run with your HEART." - Anonymous.

"She never seemed shattered; to me, she was a breathtaking mosaic of the battles she's won." -Matt Baker

"Nature is ever teeming with life: and all is seed, and all is fruit."
-Friedrich Schiller

"Though she be but little, she is fierce."
					~ William Shakespeare

"We yearn for the beautiful, the unknown, and the mysterious."
- Issey Miyake

"To all the girls that think you're fat because you're not a size zero, you're the beautiful one, its society who's ugly." - Marilyn Monroe

"Gracefulness has been defined to be the outward expression of the inward harmony of the soul." - William Hazlitt

"My goal is to be filthy rich. Rich in adventure, in health, in knowledge, in laughter, in family, and in love."
- Anonymous

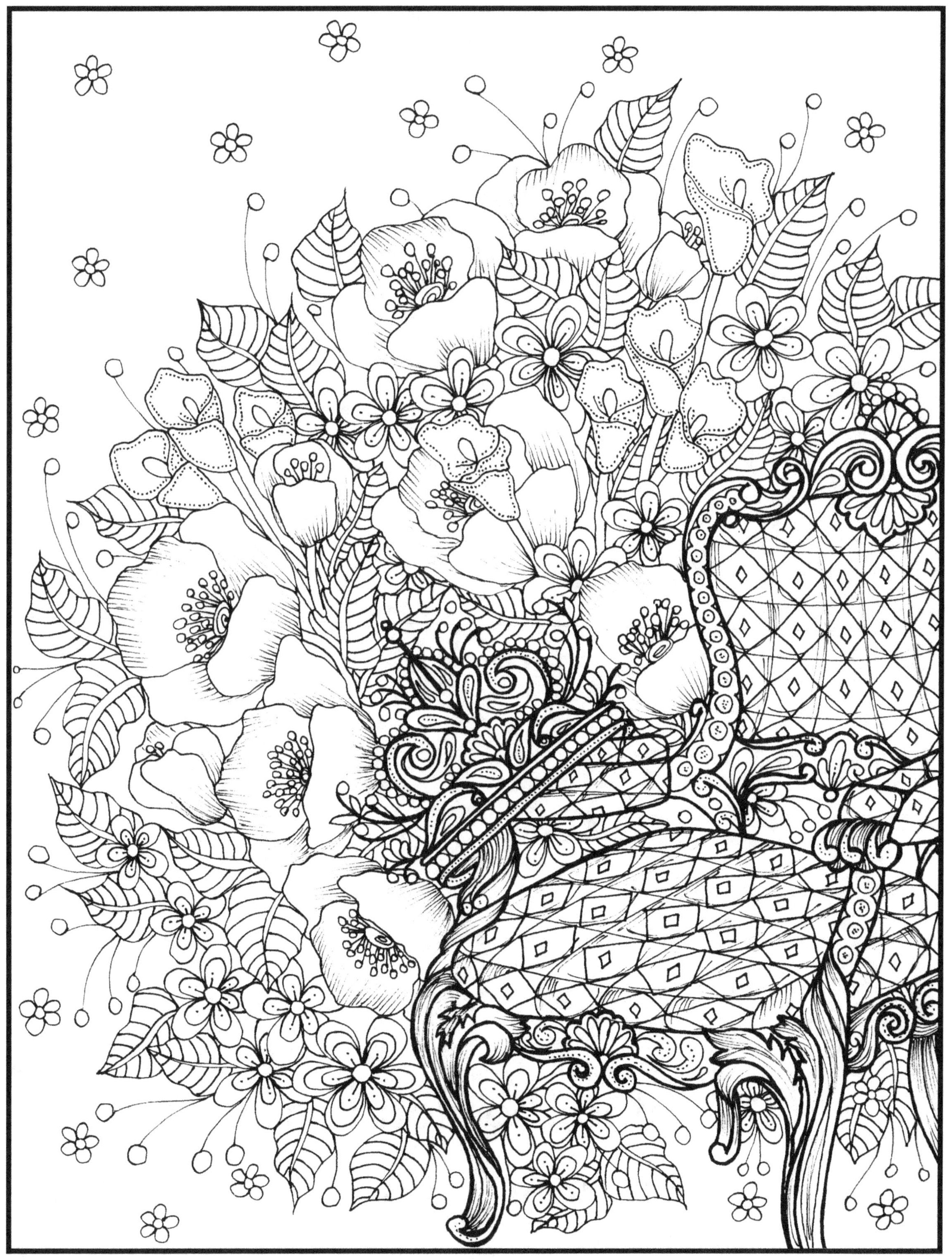

"Behind the cloud the sun is still shining." – Abraham Lincoln

"Smell the sea, and feel the sky. let
your soul and spirit fly."
- Van Morrison

"The next time your core beliefs are challenged, try being curious instead of furious." - Randy Gage

"Do not go where the path may lead,
go instead where there is no path and
leave a trail." - Ralph Waldo Emerson

"You can be the ripest, juiciest peach in the world, and there's still going to be somebody who hates peaches."
- Dita Von Teese .

"The eyes are useless when the mind is blind." - Anonymous

"I'm not afraid of storms, for I'm
learning how to sail my ship."
- Louisa May Alcott

"The wheel that squeaks the loudest is
the one that gets the grease."
-Josh Billings

"The elevator to success is out of order. You'll have to climb the stairs… One step at a time." – Joe Girard

"The bird who dares to fall, is the bird who learns to fly." - Anonymous

"A family doesn't need to be perfect; it just needs to be united." - Anonymous

"Happiness can be found, even in the darkest of times, if one only remembers to turn on the light." - Harry Potter and the Prisoner of Azkaban

"We create a mask to meet the masks of others. Then we wonder why we cannot love, and why we feel so alone."
- Brenda Shoshanna

About the Artist

Surabhi has had a flair for drawing illustrations from early years of her childhood. Surabhi believes that art can be seen in everything and anything. She believes that an artist is born with a beautiful heart and mind. "I see happiness around myself and that is what I like to draw. Creating art is like meditation to me, it relaxes and rejuvenates me." quotes Surabhi.

Intrikate Ink is her Fifth coloring book to be published, preceded by Blissful Blooms, Positive Paisleys, Mandala Mantra 1 and Mandala Mantra 2

Please share a picture of the colored pages on Instagram with #IntrikateInk and stand a chance to win a free copy of the artist's next coloring book.